Infra-Thin-Press

Copyright © 2025 Infra-Thin Press. All rights reserved.

ISBN 979-8-90148-114-1

Printed in the United States of America.

For queries or information, please contact the publisher at info@infrathinpress.com

The Pleistocene Sea

T.D. Tucker

"To romanticize the world is to make us aware of the magic, mystery and wonder of the world; it is to educate the senses to see the ordinary as extraordinary, the familiar as strange, the mundane as sacred, the finite as infinite."
— Novalis

"Keep some room in your heart for the Unimaginable."
— Mary Oliver

"The soul knows: the sea, too, must rise in revolt so it doesn't die standing still."
— Phoenix Moon

"In my work I try to look at ordinary things quite closely to see if there isn't a little bit of something special about them. I'm trying to make something as nearly perfect as I can out of words."
— Ted Kooser

mirrors of empire

the corner bar sweats stale beer
under a dingy ceiling of fluorescent gods
who can never save us.
outside the rain is a riotous mob
washing graffiti into slogans.
sewers choke on last night's protests.
signs and paper flags spill into the gutter.
the homeless man's ticking off
about hunger in the belly of his rich city.

from a saxophone's bent spine
comes a straightened note.
the drummer slides along the skin of the snare
and settles into a secret rhythm.
we all pretend to hear it because
the beat knows what the empire hides.

Old Poet

The stream brims
with rainbow trout.

The donkey cart
full of apples.

Cranes glide low
over a wild meadow,

where a peacock
sounds for his mate.

The old poet sits
in the grass,

listening to the trout
burbling in the brook,

watching sailors
on the lake
practice turning
their boats into the wind.

Later that evening,
after a supper
of roasted elk
and baked apples,

he will write a poem
about it all.

It will be
a good poem.

Quiet and true.

The Other Side

Once, driving through a roundabout in a blizzard, I signaled right and exited into a snowbank. The windshield cracked, and the steering wheel withdrew behind an airbag. I sat like a photograph behind glass. The other side of the snowbank is an ocean. On the shore, a half-submerged rowboat with a broken oar lock. The shoreline is another country. A kingdom of seaweed.

The Edge of the Fold

A shadow slips between the walls,
silence spun in whispers of glass.
The sky trembles like a leaf in the wind,
fragments of time scattered,
folding back on themselves.

My name and yours
sunk in an arctic of moments,
where the sun hordes its secrets
and the earth keeps turning without sound.

But the light—
it comes,
untouched,
through the cracks of the closed door,
silent as a bird
lifting from the dark.

The night speaks in stones
holding its breath.
In the silence,
the stones remember
the weight of lost names.

I walk through the night,
each step a new shape of time,
each thought a shadow cast
on the stony curves of distant worlds.

I could reach for the stars,
but my hands are full of rain,
and my mouth is silent
with the taste of salt and ash.

Beneath my feet,
the earth listens
with the patience of sorrow.
And you—
you are not far,
but your absence

is a mirror
I carry with me.

Somewhere,
the stars sigh
a psalm forgotten
but the wind, like a lover's final breath,
still whispers:
"Remember,
remember,
you are both lost
and found."

At dusk, the earth exhales.
The river carries yesterday's light.
I stand where two trees forget themselves,
the leaves humming with quiet urgency.

The air sinks like a drawn breath—
The clock ticks louder
when no one is here.
Time slows.

The earth whispers beneath me,
its roots deeper than memory.
I think of all that it has held:
rain, frost, snow,
a carpenter grappling with his tools.

Tonight I will dream of walking backward,
undoing each footprint,
until I reach the place where the stony path
began,
a place the map forgot to mark,
a place that hums like the river.

Beneath the vault of heaven
where rivers weave their silver hymns,
I wander, lost yet whole,
a vessel filled with drifting stars.

The earth holds me

in her fragrant arms.
Her breath is the song of pines,
her voice the murmur of streams
that fall like prayers into the open sea.

Yet even now,
as twilight presses against my chest,
I hear the echo of finitude.
It stirs the wind,
it bends the grass,
it kindles the spirit of a weary heart.
It calls me by names I've never spoken,
words that bloom only in silence:
it carries them all,
like wind through an orchard.

Time, a whisper folded beneath the
floorboards,
like the turning of leaves,
drawing the world anew.
There is only now.

The air is heavy with waiting.
What waits?
Not the end, but the space before it.

A door opens inward,
but no one enters.
The wind moves through the room,
an unwritten sentence,
its syntax carved in dust
on the sill of a forgotten window.

What are we
but the echo of stones
worn smooth by a river
that refuses to name itself?
I carry these moments—
a sparrow's wing,
the scrape of the moon against the horizon—
as if they might matter.

Who are we now,
in the breath between stones?

And still, the door stays open.
The wind whispers again,
this time more clearly:
"Nothing is yours,
but everything is given."

I Look at You

Your eyes blue flower beacons
pollinated by starlight.

Your hair breathes blue vapor.
Your lips a coral reef.

I kiss your mouth
and I am marooned.

Every star has a corner of wild darkness
where we can make love on a bed of starfish.

Lighthouses swim by us in the night sky.
Light bends around you.

a geography of silence

sitting on the fire escape
lost, in a geography of silence,

i remember my last sip of coffee
and think about my breath

smelling like coffee,
wondering if that last sip of coffee

smelled like my breath,
before it reached my lips.

and why not go on believing,
with the irony of eyes or carravagio's

tears, that the bottle knows the taste of the
wine, the paper the weight of the

words, the clay the smell of the sun,
    or the geyser the sound of the sky.

In Front of the Church

I stand.

Waiting
for the cup of yesterday
to be emptied.

A name carved
on a pew
I am no longer called.

The absence of God
is everywhere.

I guess
the day of my death,

and hope
I am right.

Day shakes
the night
with exhaustion.

I will not enter
the church.

Where mists of misery
hide the truth.

Where the walls
grip the abyss

and crosses
are covered
in the ashes
of resurrection.

Where I fear
being strangled
by a dying star.

Standing

Standing in front of the virgin mirror,
she sees tugboats towing icebergs through the forest
and seabirds sleeping in the mouths of wolves,
trees walking through a wet meadow.

She sees
the celluloid of despair and the broken
buckle holding up the earth, glaciers calving
new seas, clouds wrapped in blue cellophane.

In her house, no one is sleeping. Windows
open their eyes, and doors refuse their glances.

The virgin mirror will never speak of her nakedness,
yet her depths will be revealed.

We Burn the Wood

We burn the wood
gathered from the forest floor,
our campfire dancing
alongside our silhouettes.

The trees gather around
to breathe the ancestral smoke,
boughs bowed, as if in prayer.

Embers whirl above our heads
like tongues of Pentecost.
Our ecstasies glow to ash.

We open the tent
and the walls rush
towards the firelight.

We climb into our Chinese lantern.
From our sleeping bags
we can hear the bones
of the forest burn.

Books never to be born.

Not even this paper
on which I write
will reveal its secret of death.

Nothing is fixed.

A City

Streetlight purrs against the glass,
a cold current threads through
cracked sidewalks and bus stop benches.

Here—
everything waits:
the man with the paper sack of rye,
a woman clutching her phone like a loaded
gun,
pigeons claiming a cornice of a brownstone.

Billboards buzz with neon songs,
while sirens punctuate
the night's half-finished sentence.

We walk in fragments,
names erased by traffic,
faces carried like backpacks
through a grid of forgetting.

Yet in a sudden pause—
a boy laughs at the echo of his mother's
stilettos
a mural flakes like gold leaf—
the city inhales,
and we remember
it is alive,
then exhales us back
into the rhythm of its zealous heart.

Between Light and Silence

The morning unfolds,
a slow-breathing tide.

Here, the world asks nothing of you
but to listen—
to the hush between the storms
to the ocean's patient hymn.

To the soft press of wind upon a wildflower.

Rooted in the quiet earth,
it lifts its face—
not for us,
but for the simple joy of being.

After Work

I take the axe

from its crooking nail,
a quiet punctuation
on the woodshed wall.

Its edge remembers
what it divided.

Apple trees fall.
Their shadows shorten,
almost human
in dying distress.

Boats Leaving at Night

The moon hangs above the waves. The wind turns once, then settles. The fishing boats leave the quay cloaked in bursts of rain. Their engines fade into the dark. People wait along the dock, hands in pockets, eyes fixed on the horizon. Tomorrow feels like a room with no door, the past like a stone in the chest. Still, somewhere inside, a small light shines. It says nothing. It is enough.

I have stayed too long on this mountain

I have stayed too long on this mountain
past summer into October half-light

listening to tree-talk and waiting.
my house in the valley is hidden

behind a spot on my hand
where cuckoos nestle and smiling

gramophones rasp and hiss.
Where lamplight is clothed in miracles.

Where paintings rain off the walls.
waiting for someone

she will never recognize,
my mother sits by the door

ringing an empty bell
and stroking her hair.

Lifeboat

Snow falls.

My dogs sniff at the snow
swirling in the air—
scents of the sky
settling
on wet muzzles
in the cold crisp of winter.

Twilight.

Leading us away
into domains
of stillness—

I am swimming
alongside a lifeboat,
its hull slamming
into the breakers.

Dots of hull paint
freckling the white foam,
like punctuation marks
in the syntax of the sea.

I swim faster, finally
taking hold of the lifeboat
like a cradle.

Climbing over the handrails,
I feel the boat's heart beating
in its rusted keel—

a pulse borrowed
from wood and steel.

Snowflakes

feather
on the icy wind.

I row
to the rhythm
of the world
in utero.

Stone and Wind

I walked the path
where no one has walked
since the snow last fell.

The earth heaves underfoot,
slow, as if burdened
by the weight of many years.

The sky looks away
as if it knows
the day will soon end.

I carried the stone
up the slope again today.
It was not heavier—
only older.

The wind had nothing to say,
but the rain is eloquent
this time of year.

A crow cracked the sky
in two black wings,

and I stood
as I have stood—
silent,
unsure if I wait
or endure.

I do not know
if the apple tree still believes

in spring.

But it stands,
as I do now.

Walking

My dogs don't care if I only walk
to lose seven pounds I gained
over winter. We all four avoid the potholes
still muddled with snow melt. They sniff the road
as if knowing something I don't.

Leaving the road, we cut through a newly ploughed
field, passing a rider-less tractor, its engine idling
like a hermit humming to himself. We meet the farmer

further afield propped against a wooden
fence post eating a ham sandwich. Without me asking
he tells me it burns less diesel to let a tractor idle
than turning its engine off then over again.

I ask what he will plant and he just shrugs,
as if knowing something we don't. He nods
towards the road, and we walk on
leaving 97 shoe prints and 3750
toe tracks in his freshly furrowed dirt.

War

The bridge we crossed
lies crumpled between stone
and sea. A swarm of jets dins up
through the silence; how the sky
curdles in the noise!

Bombs again.
Cell phone towers
go dead. There's no
electricity since yesterday
and the gulls are quiet.

Storm

By the time I reached the cellar
the storm had passed,
sirens drifting east.

The corrugated door, red paint
crackled like gold leaf
on a Bronze age urn,
was still there, half-hinged.

Anyway, it was still
locked since last winter.

Our house looked dazed.
Pea sized drops of hail
drained through the gutter
spouts like frozen tears, rattling
as they rolled out.

The sun quit its reticence
and sputtered, shattering
a poplar into shards
of purple shadow flung
against the house.

The window panes
abruptly lit and you too
lit up in one.

By then the sky seemed
marooned
in a sea of yellow
and the house no
longer quivered.

Cinders

The stars perform
their computations:
they measure,
they trace,
they fold
the night
over the fields.

Night stretches.
It offers a path
full of language,
but no words.

Epistles in cinders
impossible to read.
Letters burned,
letters lost.
Silent.
Still.

Roundabout

Bone marrow
barely
chugging
along—

hemoglobin
gobbling
small bits
of O_2

speeding
through a roundabout
with
no exit.

Nothing
to be done
but love,
be loved,
and die.

Today
is
my favorite
day.

Coyowolf

Pulling the car over
to the asphalt shoulder,

studded here and there
with prairie dog scat,

we watch the coyote—
K-9 sized—
cross Hwy 385.

"That's no coyote,
that's a wolf."
Katy says.

"But there are no wolves
in South Dakota."

Perhaps she wandered down
from pine-forested Minnesota,

ranging west
through Buffalo Gap,
lapping at French Creek along the way,

or, loping out of Yellowstone,
made tracks south and east
for Harney Peak,

crossed Medicine Bow,
camouflaged
in a coyote pelt.

Paying our talk no mind,
the coyowolf trotted off,

rambling through the rhizome
of red blackberry brambles,

before disappearing
into a great stand
of aspen wood.

Love's Sorrow

I will wait for August,
to see my home again—
open windows streaked by bird strikes,
ladders leaning on half painted walls.

I can no longer pause
to break the yellow yoke of despair.

I am drawing near
to the last eclipse,
where love reduces itself
to a sliver of leaden light—

In each hand,
a cup of tomorrow,
earth and sky twined
on a white tablecloth—
a still life of unfinished futures.

Glances fall
from the ceiling of past lives,
while shadows seek shade
in the void,

The blue moon
breaks over tepid rocks,
and I am moving away
from languishing landscapes—
the slow decay of distance
Away from the paper faces
of forgotten lovers
and the handshake of sorrow.

I, too,
am forgotten—
fading in the fold.

The Motorcycle Mechanic

You left the University in 'eighty-two,
and that was when I lost you to that motorcycle
mechanic. Although I wished you well, I secretly
desired that bastard would collide full force
against a stone wall on a winding road.
And then I'd follow you into the hall
of some dim hospital, where you could lean
and cry against my shoulder without shame.

When they had turned the life support machine
off at his bedside, I would take you out
to lunch inside a café where the menu
listed each living creature from the sea.
I'd warn you not to order the *dauphin*;
despite its name, it doesn't taste like dolphin.

I would present myself at his funeral
as solemn, though I'd feel a quiet joy
inside me knowing he was finally gone,
and glad that you and I might find a way
to be together once again. In time
your grief would subside. We would marry then
within the very church where, years before,
the lid had closed upon his coffin's frame
and shut him from the world forevermore.

Japanese Dogwood

A lone Japanese Dogwood,
Treeing on its mountain.

Chirps

They chirp in rhymes,
        these crickets,
rhyming sonnets to the moon.

Trees are treeing,
                    as trees do,

                                      rooting
for the crickets.

There is frost riming around tree

                trunks.

There are broken bells
Disguised as pinecones.

No birds are singing.
It's night, and
they are sleeping.
                      Dreaming rhyming
cricket songs.

Reveries of Emile Cioran

Decay, not decadence. A triptych of blue mollusks rests in the attics of memory. Optic revolution passes, then the hush of history settles. Cioran's tongue moves like a seeing machine through pale white glass. Tortuous poets, arthritic verses petrified by frenzy, gather at the feet of certitude. They carry a fetish for the sidewalk, for the grave, and wander the canyons of deserted books. Vanishing, they drift through the gardens of Luxembourg. Legends sit in blue shade, stranded, laughing. A veil of uncertainty falls, and they return.

Art of Ruin

I have been
to museums in Italy.

I laughed
at the art of ruin—
saints on ceilings,
plundered Gods.

Heaven lit
from above.

God hiding
behind two blades of grass.

Jesus crucified
in the Piazza del Duomo,
robed
in the finery
of a Tuscan Prince.

I have seen the past
in the ruins of the present.

Frescos fading
behind the yellow varnish
of yesterday.

I have followed
the marble footprints
of Roman statues

to dead ends,

felt the sword blow
of Caravaggio,

and eyed triptychs of a
virgin

After the Storm

The storm carved a mile-wide path through the swamp, flattening nearly three-quarters of the hardwood trees that stood between cattails and the tall summer grass. Tourist families climbed out of their RVs and campers to stare at the crowds wading in disbelief through the rising water. Others walked slowly through the fallen colonnades of cottonwoods and planted pines, searching for pieces of their former lives or for the small spring that used to bubble out of the swamp floor.

In the middle of this wreckage, they found her. She was straining to lift a black-and-white television—the kind with rabbit-ear antennas—that had been buried under two feet of mud at the bottom of the shallow swamp. As she dug it out, the brown muck around the set shifted into an eerie gray glow, and people drew closer, startled by the light that rose from the murky water. When she finally cleared the last of the mud, the crowd saw that the television, though unplugged and half-drowned, was somehow still on. It was broadcasting a live episode of *Praise the Lord* in crisp tones of black and white.

Everyone who saw it felt marked by the moment. Tourists and locals alike were baptized in the swamp that day. The tourists went home and sold their RVs and campers, sending the money to TBN. The locals promised they would do the same as soon as their insurance checks arrived.

Chokecherries

You bring your prized bull
back to the barn at first frost.
The hay is cut and dried
and baled and young steers
follow you to the stock tank
leaving hoof prints in the frost.

The days hang on.

There are still bands of chokecherries
behind your house, potatoes
to be dug up, clusters of monarchs
feasting on milkweed
and your neighbor's lambs
graze along the fence. Drones float
around the beehives.

Soon the sun will rut,
with elk and magpies
drunk on chokecherry drupes,
red beaks a dead giveaway.

From your kitchen window you watch
and laugh
as they stumble around the yard.

You have the good sense to join them,
sipping from a bottle of homemade wine.

Suppers are less lonely
in such company.

I Won't Complain

I won't
          complain
about the drip
                            drip
                                  drip
of the leaky

kitchen faucet
if
     you stop
grumbling about
                     the cold   cold   cold
drafts wafting through
                        the house

dead leaves   and
                                   insects clog
the gutters   and deer droppings

like bits of bird song litter our yard   but the cricket's

      chirp
chirp   chirp

reminds   us

                                                   of sleep

In the Old World

In the old world
the Iroquois clans
paddled three days
against the river
upstream just to exchange
greetings with friends.
At dusk
someone lifts an arm
and birch boats
are beached
on some jut of land.

The women cut
long leafy boughs
from fledgling pines.
Soon the shelters
lean into the same
stripped saplings.

Meat is roasted.

Songs of thanks
are sung
voices mingling
in smoky blue hues.

In the morning
they take the branches,
carry them back
to the birch canoes,
and shove off—
leaving nothing

but moccasin prints
at the waterline.

Sometimes
the simplest offering
is made
from the earth itself.

The Mill

The watermill taught the river which way to flow. Does anyone remember when it was built? It's in ruin now, stone walls crumbling, and the millstone hauled away. The brewers have all moved north to buy barley from mechanized granaries.

It's March. The bears and otters, swimming in the old millrace, and the blueberry bushes on the bank have a misunderstanding. The otters eat the blueberries, and the bears eat the otters. Hunters shoot, then eat the bears.

Winter has finally withered, like the fig tree Jesus cursed. Monarch caterpillars lunch on milkweed. In ten days, we will return to the river to find the souls of lost children fluttering in the mulberries.

Journey of a Deerhound on the High Plains

I.

Custer lay dead, yet Rosie could not know.
He is sprawled face-down, his left cheek pressed in dirt
clotted dark with blood. One mortal wound
was tunneled through his back; another drilled
clean through his skull. His horse named Vic lay still,
mouth dripping red, his nostrils clogged with blood,
a fallen beast who seemed as lifeless too.
She'd seen men shot, and horses torn by guns,
and dogs with arrows piercing ragged hides,
but never yet her master fallen so still.
His luck had always held. She lowered her head
toward where his breath should move and sniffed the air.
The grass below lay cold without a trace of breath.
She nosed the wound that marked his blood-soaked back
and pushed his shoulder gently with her paw,
yet nothing stirred. She licked along his ear,
then brushed her tongue across the rigid mouth—
but he lay mute, unmoving as the dawn.

II.

She heard an arrow whistle from behind
before she saw its point. She sprang ahead,
then turned in time to watch it bite the earth,
to auger down and vanish in the dust.
She wheeled leftward and saw swift He Crow run
uphill, a second arrow set and still,
unquivering and ready for the string.
Then Rosie hopped across dead Custer's form
and fled in leaps, in bounding, broken darts,
in zigzags through the brambles and the strewn
and stiffened bodies scattered on the slope,
until she heard no more his footfalls strike
the chalky butte where Custer's body lay.
She paced the summit just beyond the range
of arrow shot, alert and watching down.
She saw He Crow strip off the whitened shirt
and tug the cavalry boots from Custer's feet.

Around them spread the prairie, littered bright
with treasury notes, poker-won, that fanned
and fluttered through the tall and shivering grass.
Then women came with long and pointed sticks
to prod his body, poke at both his ears,
and cut away thin strands of yellow hair.
At this, she growled, then whimpered in her throat,
and howled once more, then turned at last to go,
and loped northeast across the next low butte,
back toward the line of distant Fort Lincoln.

III.

Rosie, born three years before at Fort Lincoln,
neither runt nor alpha, was third of eight pups.
Her father was a purebred deerhound bred
for size and speed; her mother carried blood
of deerhound, Irish wolfhound, and a trace
of greyhound in the cross. Her long, straight legs,
her deep, wide chest, and slim but heavy bones
could let a stranger take her for a purebred.
Her high-set ears lay folded back like those
of greyhounds, angled over hazel eyes
dark-rimmed with shadow. And her muzzle stretched
in narrow taper to a blue-black nose.
Her rough coat mixed in brindle shades of gray
along her head and neck and through her mane,
then brightened into white across her chest,
her belly, and the lower legs she used
to chase all things that moved. Her tail hung low,
half-tucked when still, its curling tip washed white.
But mutt or not, she lived and moved as hound.

Custer would travel with a forty-dog
companion pack on high-plains campaigns west.
They followed every turn he made, and he
would often break from column on a whim,
ride hard toward some butte, drop out of sight,
and only the far echo of the pack
gave any hint of where he'd gone or why—
until he rose again along the ridge
with dogs behind. His men despised these acts,

his restless need to prove himself, but Rosie
thrived on the chaos. Of the pack, she ran
the fastest, and she slept beside his bedroll
curled in the canvas warmth of army cloth.
She ate the first of all the dogs and joined
his morning rides before the bugles called.
Out on the plains, she felt as free as wolves.
On June the twenty-fifth, he gave the order
that every dog remain behind the mules,
but Rosie stood beside Vic's hooves already
before he ever knew she'd slipped the line.

She looked northeast. She knew the broken land
the Sioux called *makhóšiča*—badlands, cliffs
of sand and canyon, toadstool rock and dust,
and scarce, thin water cutting barren stone,
the layers crumbling into ash and silt.
Custer adored this landscape for the ways
it met him harshly, how it never asked
for gentleness, how blunt its terms could be.
He rode straight through whenever he was given
a chance to spare the column a retreat
around its edges. Rosie'd run the cuts
and ridges with him many times, had chased
the sudden skirmishes he stirred with anyone
caught peaceably along his chosen path—
but she had never crossed the badlands solo.

She sniffed the air for any of her pack,
but found no scent. She raised her right front paw,
pulled out a goat head burr between her toes,
and spat it from her tongue. She sniffed again,
her gaze following the horned larks flickering
above the heavy tassels of the grass.
She started walking with the fading sun
pressed to her back. After two hours she stopped.
The light was nearly gone. She turned three times
to flatten down the grass and lay to sleep.

She woke before the dawn. Though nearly dark,
her eyes adjusted to the faint, gray wash
of prairie light. She rose and stretched herself

in low, long arcs, then settled down again.
The bed of matted grass held warmth, but all
the prairie felt cold-slick with morning dew.
She lowered to the grass and licked the beads,
then rose and didn't wander far to find
a place apart to urinate. She stretched,
returned, and licked her lips and yawned again
and soon was back asleep. She was awakened

by the damp, sharp scent of antelope.
She leapt to stand and saw the herd nearby,
no more than fifty yards away. She poised
to chase, but the antelope pricked their ears,
looked straight at her, and bolted in a wave
through tallgrass bending in one fluent sweep.
She watched the bluestem parting in the wind
until they reached the sandstone on the rise
a mile ahead. She raised her head and loped
toward the rising sun. It was still low

when she first smelled the water. Cottonwoods
rose up around a shallow, winding coulee
that carved beneath a bluff of sunbaked sand.
She crossed the bank and pressed her paws in deep,
then waded in up to her cooling chest
and drank the river in slow, steady laps,
her ears half-tilted, listening for change.
A high-pitched sound rang out downstream. She froze,
her ears now angled sharply to the bend.
She looked and saw a shape along a bar
just out of view. One final drink, then Rosie
moved to shore in splashing strides and ran
toward the distant sandbar, fording through
a shallow riffle just above the fork
where river let the bar rise from its floor.
Before she could make out the shape by sight,
she smelled the dying horse. On reaching him,

she saw him on his side, his head half-lifted,
nostrils blowing bubbles in the mud

like tiny bursts from silt and standing pools.
She paced in nervous arcs and then drew close
to where the wound between the withers bled,
a small, round hole that gurgled when he breathed
and bubbled as he forced the air back out.
She whimpered once and stepped across his legs,
sniffed at his snuffling nostrils, licked his face.
And when she looked again into his eyes
she saw herself reflected there and knew—
this was the horse called Chestnut, one she'd heard
the day before, six lengths behind her master
when Custer charged the village on his bay.

A motion caught her eye: a jackrabbit
had hopped into a puddle just to drink.
She stiffened, ready to explode in chase,
but then it vanished in the brush. She dropped
onto her belly, haunches raised, her muzzle
resting across the horse's trembling neck.
She listened to his breathing slow, then slow
again, until the final rhythm failed.
She felt the pulsing fade beneath her jaw
and knew at last that Chestnut's life was gone.

She stayed until the sun climbed overhead.
Her stomach rumbled. Lifting from his neck,
she licked his ears, then turned toward the river.
Upstream, across an eddy shaded blue
behind a boulder, she could see the trout
rise up to catch the insects on the film.
Most dogs can't fish, but Rosie learned by watching
the grizzly cubs along the Yellowstone.
She crossed the river toward the grassy bank,
crept through the low brush, reentered upstream,
and let the current drift her silently
until she reached the boulder's shadowed side.
Then balanced on a ledge no wider than
her outstretched paw, she watched the pool below—
its surface holding colors of the stones
in wavering shapes of blue and gray and beige.
A mallard landed far downstream, then rose,
its shadow flickering across the pool

in broken bars of wings. Then suddenly
a cutthroat breached, its open mouth engulfing
a drifting mayfly. As its body sank,
she swept her paw across the lateral line
and hooked it clean, then bit the thrashing weight
until it stilled and carried it uphill
to eat atop the stone. When she was done,
she caught two more and ate until she felt
her hunger settle. She roused at dawn
upon the boulder, warmed by rising heat.
She licked the empty spot where she had fed
and found a scrap of bone or fish-skin left.
She stood and looked downstream and saw again
the dead horse lying on the sandbar's edge.
She shook her coat; the water-beads rose up
around her head and vanished in the air.
Then Rosie leapt and swam toward the bank.

She trotted fast through switchgrass, soapweed stands,
and stopped at times to pull a burr from paw
or judge the better route around a briar.
By afternoon she reached a high plateau
where she could see a narrow plain below
enclosed by hoodoos capped in limestone crust
and shallow gullies cut from ancient flow
long drained and lost. And from that height she saw
a long, slow-moving cloud of dust, its tail
thin as a tadpole tapering behind
Sitting Bull and the Hunkpapas moving north
toward Canada. Below them on the flats
she glimpsed another trail that curved northeast
around the red and black mudstone and hill.
She scrambled down the bluff through broken shale
until she reached the dry, warm sand below.
Her nose dropped to the ground; she found the scent
of men and horses mixed, a faint trace too
of dogs who'd passed before. And when the smell
grew strongest, she looked up and recognized
the broad, worn track that led toward Fort Lincoln.
She turned and trotted down the path she knew.

Night gathered. Rosie walked a long, long way
retracing what she'd crossed days earlier.
The land seemed emptied out—no antelope
except at distance, no prairie dogs, no sign
of horses, men, or dogs—only the faint
and fading scents that lingered where they passed.

IV.

Rosie stirred along the creek's west bank.
The scent of sage mixed with the dampened air
of ponderosa pine and juniper
drew her downhill into a small arroyo
where she could crouch and quietly relieve
the tightening pressure in her morning gut.
She nudged a pine cone, turned it with her nose
to take its scent, then sniffed the dampened ring
it printed in the grass before she left
and trotted back toward the creek's soft edge.

Standing beside the water, looking south,
she saw the mesa she had crossed before—
its rocky outcrops sharp against the sky.
She waded in but kept the depth below
her chest, then paused when something caught her eye:
a torn straw hat hung on a low-set branch
above an eddy swirling under shade.
She swam across and sniffed it once, then dropped
her interest when she saw a crayfish drift
across the pebbles on the creek's clear bed.
She breathed in quick and plunged her head beneath,
her right paw scooping up the spiny shell.
Before she rose, her jaws had crushed its back,
the twitching legs like extra teeth that scraped
against her lips until she swallowed whole.
Half walking, half afloat, she found a few more
and ate them too. Although the crayfish filled
her hunger briefly, soon she felt the sick:
a slow turn inside her gut. She sought out grass
and chewed the coarse green blades until she gagged,
brought up the meal, then drank from the cold creek,

and lay upon the muddy bank to cool
her belly in the shallow, silty run.

She faced the north. Across the creek, she saw
a single buffalo begin to move,
its silhouette slow-shifting on the plain.
Behind it followed low, persistent dust,
a cloud that hugged the ground and built in size.
Then other specks appeared in scattered clumps,
and suddenly the dust began to rise.
To her far east another swelling cloud
pushed outward from a stand of mulberry
and drifted toward the first. She saw faint glints—
the dull metallic flash of something struck
by angled sun—and then she heard a sound
like distant thunder rolling over stone.
For moments, both slow clouds of dust converged,
then wavered, thinned, and finally fell apart.
The second cloud dissolved into a wisp
that drifted upward, vanished into blue.
And when the haze had cleared, she saw again
the soft-edged forms of men who moved around
the place the buffalo had grazed before.
They rode on horseback. From the distant glare,
she could not know if they were Indian bands
or soldiers hunting buffalo for meat.

All Living Things

We see ourselves
in an ant's black eyes.

We hear our voices
in the wolf's howl.

A part of us
is in the silence of the wind.

The mossy whispers
at the pond's edge
are trees speaking
a language
we once knew
and will learn again.

We fathom the depth
of an elephant's grief,
the logic of crows,
compassion for
a blade of grass.

The sun will rise.
We vibrate in
brief concord with
all living things.

www.ingramcontent.com/pod-product-compliance
Lightning Source LLC
Chambersburg PA
CBHW061419090426
42743CB00027B/3498